mainstreaming the hearing impaired child: an educational alternative

by

janice zatzman orlansky

thomas n. fairchild
series editor

danial b. fairchild
thomas n. fairchild
illustrators

Teaching Resources Corporation
100 Boylston Street, Boston, Massachusetts 02116, 617-357-8446

Library of Congress Cataloging in Publication Data

Orlansky, Janice Zatzman.
    Mainstreaming the hearing impaired child.

    (Mainstreaming series)
    Bibliography: p.
    1.   Deaf—Education.   I.   Title.
HV2430.066   371   7658501
ISBN 0-89384-011-4

Teaching Resources Corporation
100 Boylston Street, Boston, Massachusetts 02116
617-357-8446 · A New York Times Company

To Michael
Tamar
And My Parents,
With Love

acknowledgments

Barbara A. McLetchie, Halifax, Nova Scotia, Canada, teacher and parent of a hearing impaired child.

Michael D. Orlansky, University of Idaho, former educational consultant for deaf-blind children, Northwest Regional Center, Seattle, Washington.

Marcy Taylor, University of Idaho, typist.

preface

In the past, the educational needs of exceptional children were met by removing them from the "mainstream" of the regular classrooms, and serving them in a variety of segregated self-contained special classes. The trend in the '70's is educating exceptional chldren in the least restrictive educational setting; that is, as close as possible to their normal peers. This concept of "mainstreaming" exceptional children has received considerable support from within and outside the educational community. Although self-contained special classes will always be a meaningful alternative for some children, the personal and educational needs of many exceptional children can better be served in the regular class program with the supportive services of ancillary personnel and/or resource room help.

With the emphasis on "mainstreaming," the regular classroom teacher is now expected to meet the needs of exceptional children in his or her classroom along with all the other children in the class. The problem is that most regular classroom teachers have little or no preparation in the area of educating exceptional children. Regular classroom teachers need basic information regarding the various exceptionalities, and more specifically, practical suggestions which they can employ to enhance the "mainstreamed" exceptional child's personal and educational development.

The MAINSTREAMING SERIES was written to fill this need. Each book in the SERIES addresses itself to one area of exceptionality allowing teachers to select from the SERIES according to their interest or need. Each text provides information designed to correct misconceptions and stereotypes, and to improve the teacher's understanding of the exceptional child's uniqueness. Numerous practical suggestions are offered which will help the teacher work more effectively with the exceptional child in the "mainstream" of the regular classroom.

Currently, there is a great deal of controversy surrounding the use of categories and labels. The books in the SERIES are organized according to categories of exceptionality because the content within each book is only relevant for a child with a specific handicapping condition. The intent is not to propagate labeling; in fact, labeling children is inconsistent with the philosophy of the SERIES. The books address themselves to behaviors, and how teachers can work with these behaviors in exceptional children. The books in the SERIES are categorized—not the children. The books are categorized in order to cue teachers to the particular content for which they might be looking.

There is much truth in the old saying, "A picture is worth a thousand words." A cartoon format was used for each book in the MAINSTREAMING SERIES as a means of sustaining interest and emphasizing important concepts. The cartoon format also allows for easy, relaxed reading. We felt that teachers, being on the firing line all day, would be more likely to read and refer to our material, than to a lengthy text filled with theory and jargon. Typically cartoons exaggerate, stereotype, and focus on weaknesses. I sincerely hope that these cartoons do not offend any children, parents, or professionals, because that is not the purpose for which they were intended. They are intended to make you think.

I hope you find this book helpful in your work with mainstreamed exceptional children, or with any other children, since they are all special.

THOMAS N. FAIRCHILD
SERIES EDITOR

contents

teaching methods
- experience trips and stories
- vocabulary
- reading
- dramatic play
- language of instruction
- music
- driver education

4. the mainstreaming story of one child

5. an ounce of prevention: early identification

6. resources can make your task easier

resource people
resource material

7. conclusion

it's a privilege

chapter 1

---

introduction

INTEGRATION - AN ADVENTURE

Clearly, mainstreaming will not be suitable for all hearing impaired students. Let's view integration as an adventure. For the hearing impaired student it may be a voyage into the unknown, and the chances are the same holds true for the regular classroom teacher.

Integration is an adventure for the hearing impaired student because it affords him or her the opportunity to be less isolated and to participate in the mainstream.

Successful mainstreaming is the result of a cooperative team effort between parents, specialized staff, regular teachers, the principal, and the community at large.

Those hearing impaired students who do qualify for mainstreaming will usually have well-developed lipreading, speech, and language skills. The hearing impaired student will need to have a realistic view of integration. He or she should be prepared to receive extra help in the regular classroom; or, if not ready for complete integration in a regular class, return to a self-contained class with other hearing impaired youngsters.

Creating a climate where experiences of success are frequent, without giving false praise, will encourage the hearing impaired student to adjust to a regular class, and will help him or her have a positive attitude and a better understanding of the teacher's expectations.

SUCCESS

The regular classroom teacher will probably want to be in contact with other professionals who have worked with the hearing impaired student. A meeting or staffing with these professionals can be helpful.

Whenever appropriate, parents should be invited to the staff meetings.

There should also be a time limit set for the staff meeting so that only the important issues are discussed.

At the end of the meeting the important points should be summarized, an outline of responsibilities delegated, and a course of action to help the student should be set into motion.

MISCONCEPTIONS

It is easy to underestimate the intellectual ability of the hearing impaired person; especially if you are unfamiliar with the profound effect a hearing loss has on the development of speech and language. I.Q. scores rely heavily on understanding language and the subtleties of language. Consequently, I.Q. scores are not an accurate guide to a hearing impaired person's intelligence.

Not all hearing impaired people:

- Use sign language

- Lipread or speechread

- Use understandable speech

- Wear hearing aids

- Can see well enough to compensate for their hearing loss

All hearing impaired people have a communication problem to some degree, either in expressing ideas or in understanding language.

INTEGRATION POSSIBILITIES

By using the terms "integration" or "mainstreaming," we are not always referring to complete integration into the regular classroom. A self-contained classroom of hearing impaired students in the regular school is also a form of integration. Any move away from complete isolation such as institutionalization is a step toward the normal and could be viewed as mainstreaming.

If you are a regular classroom teacher and your school has a classroom of hearing impaired children, you might approach the teacher of that class and ask if one or two children could join your class for an activity. Suggested first activities could be a birthday party, . . .

. . .gym class, or teaching the rules of a game. Hearing impaired children often have great difficulty in comprehending the unwritten rules of children's games so it is necessary to explain the rules more graphically. By observing the game or activity first, the hearing impaired student will better understand what is expected from each child when participating.

Later, if the hearing impaired student is prepared to join your class for a lesson in an academic subject, he or she could do so on a part-time basis. The special education teacher and the regular classroom teacher should be in constant communication with each other regarding the hearing impaired student's progress in order for complete or partial integration to be effective.

In exchange for your time with the hearing impaired student, perhaps the special education teacher could take a few of your students. Initially the exchange could be social. . .

. . .and later the special education teacher might want to explain about hearing aids and answer questions. A tutorial arrangement, where the hearing student assists the hearing impaired student, could also be organized. The hearing impaired student could also share certain skills with the hearing students, such as teaching signs and fingerspelling to interested hearing students. It is advisable to have this exchange take place between children of the same age.

WHAT CAUSES A HEARING LOSS?

Basically there are two types of hearing loss:

1. Conductive hearing loss

2. Sensori-neural hearing loss

A conductive hearing loss involves some kind of blockage such as impacted wax or infection in the middle ear.

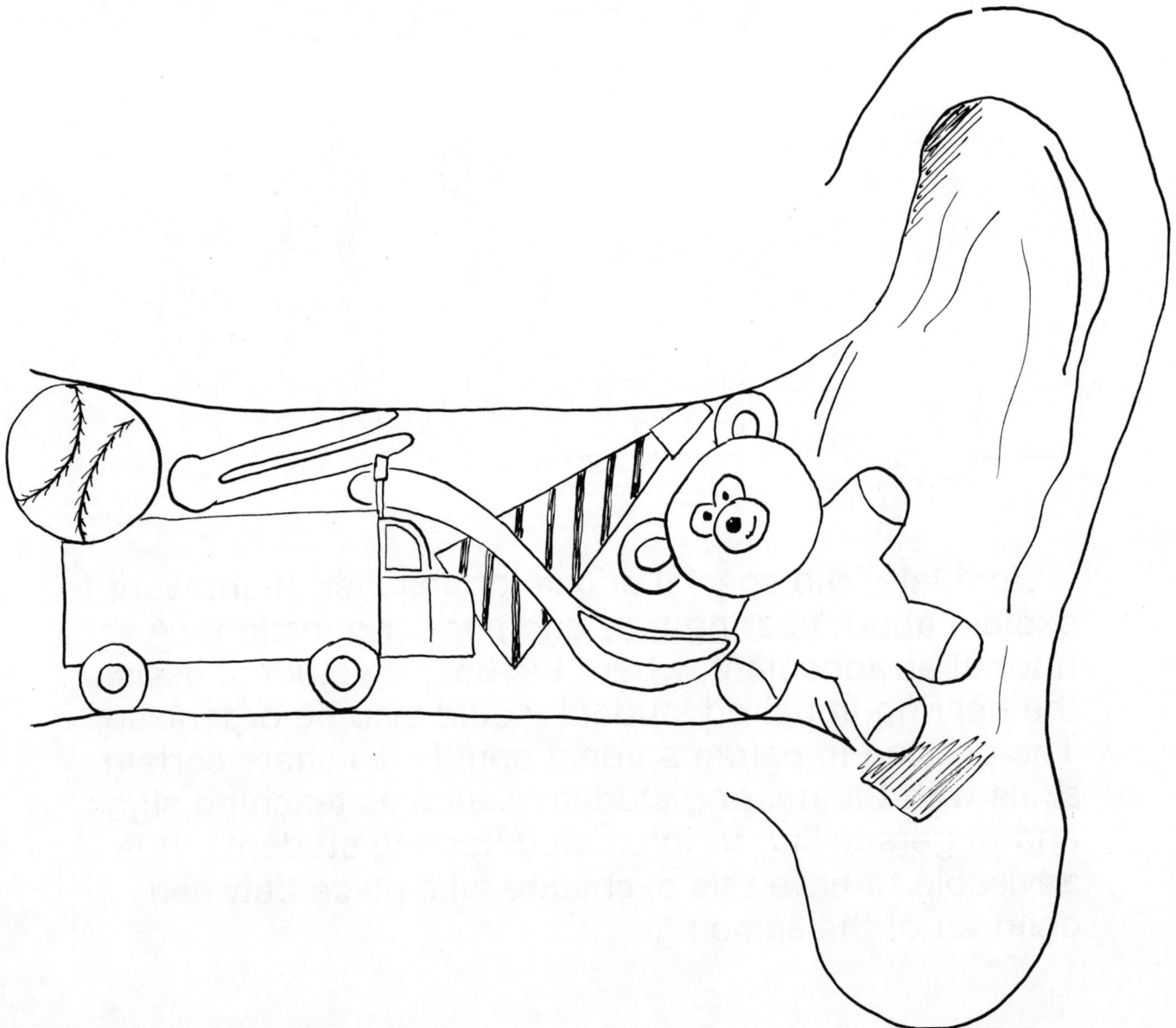

A conductive hearing loss can also be due to a congenital malformation, such as an absence of the outer ear. This malformation may be associated with damage to the deeper structures in the ear.

A conductive hearing loss can quite often be corrected by surgery.

A sensori-neural hearing loss implies damage to the 'sensors' or nerve fibers which connect the inner ear to the hearing center in the brain. Since damaged nerve fibers do not regenerate or repair themselves like some other parts of the body, the damage is permanent, so at present surgery cannot correct the hearing loss.

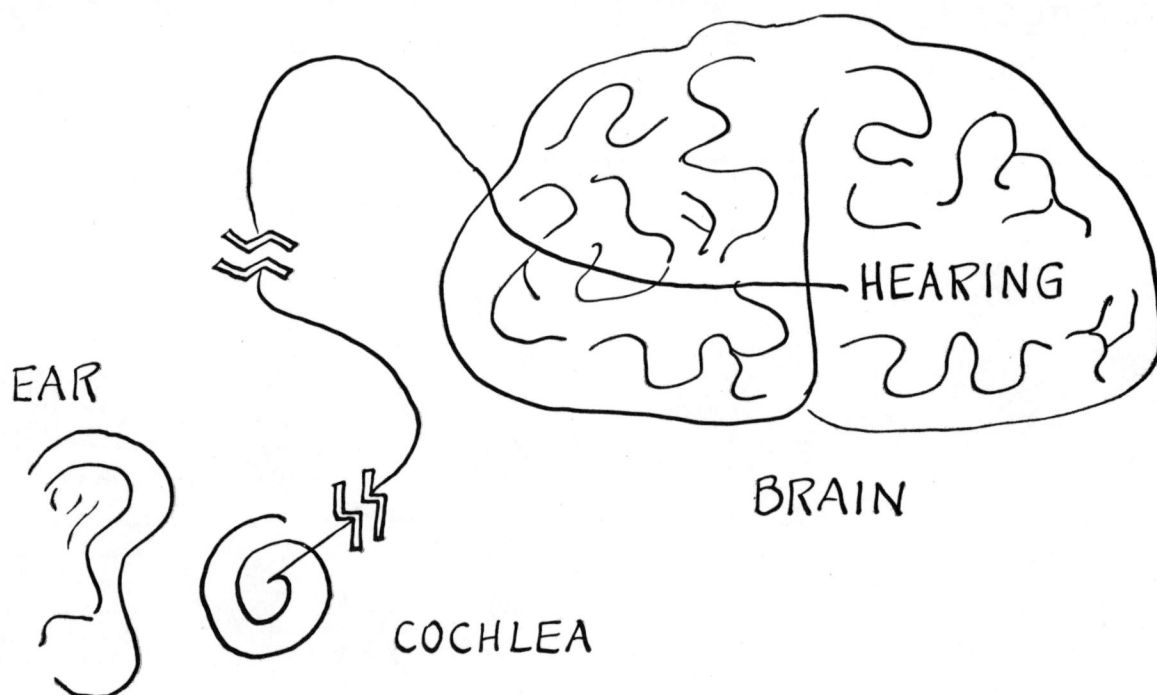

EAR

HEARING

BRAIN

COCHLEA

Possible causes of a sensori-neural hearing loss are: heredity; drugs; permanent damage due to excessive noise; mother having had rubella or german measles in first trimester of pregnancy; RH factor incompatibility at birth; meningitis; and some infectious diseases, such as the mumps.

chapter 2

---

terminology

DEFINITIONS

An Audiologist is a person trained to test levels of hearing by using various types of equipment. The audiologist graphs the findings from these tests on an audiogram.

An Audiogram is a graph that shows the level of hearing. (Example on page 18.)

A Hearing Aid is a small machine that is used to amplify sound. However, it does not make sounds clearer so supervised practice is necessary before one can make effective use of this aid.

Hearing Impaired is a general term indicating some malfunction of the auditory mechanism. **Deaf** implies the hearing impairment is severe and hearing alone may not be sufficient for language comprehension. Therefore, another mode(s) of communication must be employed by the deaf person. **Hard of Hearing** refers to an individual whose hearing loss is sufficient to require either amplification or remedial help in communication skills. Usually speech is their major means of conversing. The hard of hearing live in a "gray world" – they cannot hear sounds clearly nor are they shut off from sounds completely.

An Otologist is a medical doctor who specializes in pathologies and treatment of the ear and surrounding areas.

Residual Hearing refers to the amount of hearing that remains after damage to the auditory mechanism. Making functional use of the residual hearing is an important objective for all those working with the hearing impaired person.

MODES OF COMMUNICATION

Fingerspelling or the Manual Alphabet consists of various finger configurations which form individual letters of the alphabet and can be strung together to make words.

An Interpreter is a person who can transmit a verbal or written message to the hearing impaired person by using one or a combination of the following: sign language, fingerspelling, speech, and residual hearing.

Lipreading or Speechreading is an acquired skill. It is used to comprehend spoken language by recognizing the meaning of the message by movements of the face, lips, throat muscles, and placement of the tongue of the speaker.

Total Communication is a means of receiving and expressing language by using a combination of the following: speech, residual hearing, fingerspelling, and sign language.

Sign Language is a system of expressing and receiving language. Various hand and body movements have been formalized to convey words, concepts and phrases. There are different systems of sign language.

Speech is an oral means of communication.

FREQUENCY (PITCH) MEASURED IN HERTZ (Hz)

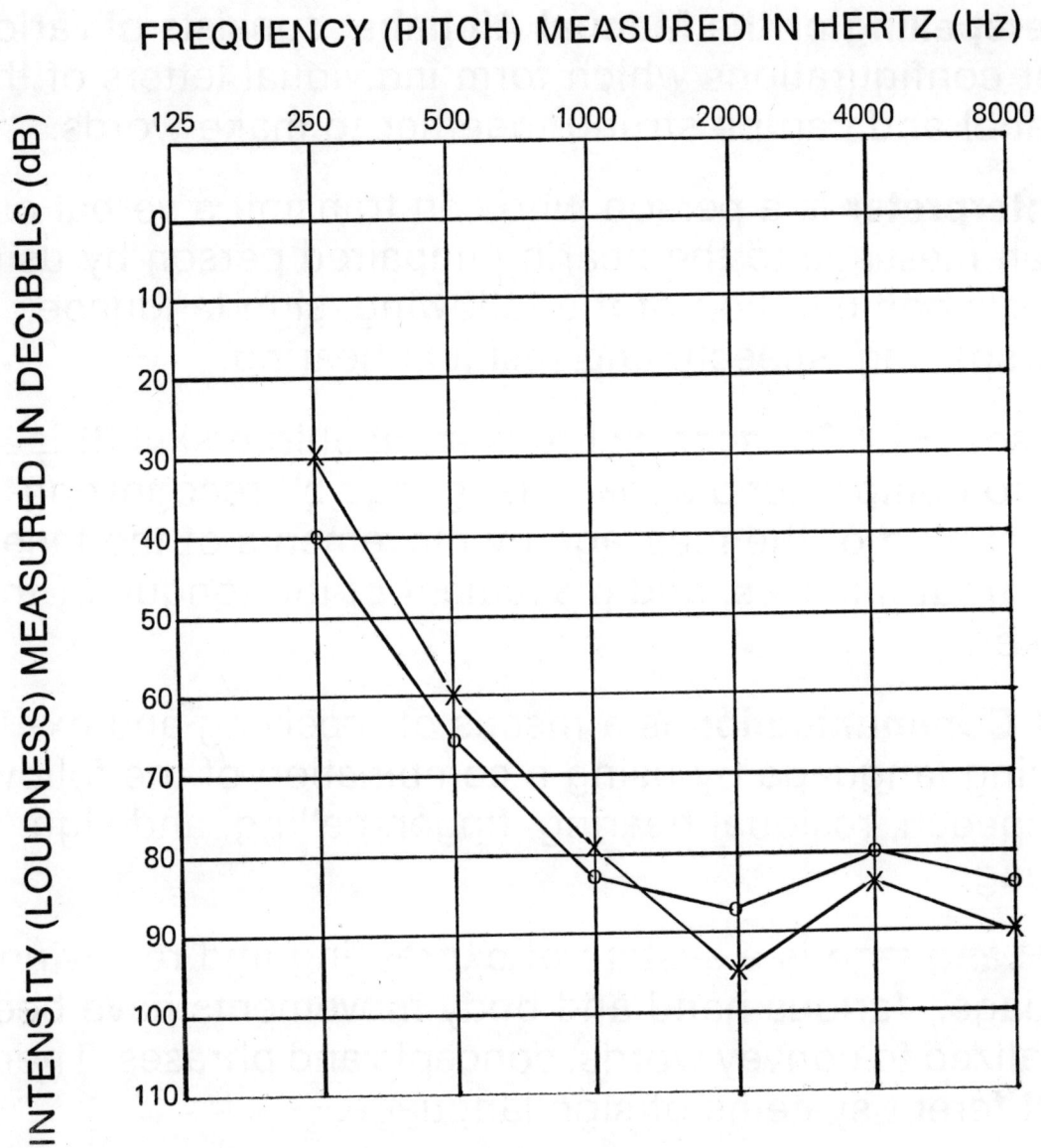

SAMPLE
AUDIOGRAM

SYMBOLS USED ON AUDIOGRAM:

	RIGHT EAR	LEFT EAR
AIR CONDUCTION	O	X
BONE CONDUCTION	[	]

NOTE: BONE CONDUCTION IS NOT MEASURED IN FREQUENCIES ABOVE 4000 Hz.

Explanation of this type of hearing loss:

The audiogram on page 18 depicts a bilateral (i.e. present in both ears) sensori-neural hearing loss which becomes more severe in the higher frequencies.

This audiogram shows that only air conduction (X, O) was used to measure the hearing loss. If there is a significant gap between the air conduction and bone conduction results, there is reason to believe a conductive hearing loss is present. Such is not the case in this audiogram.

MANUAL ALPHABET

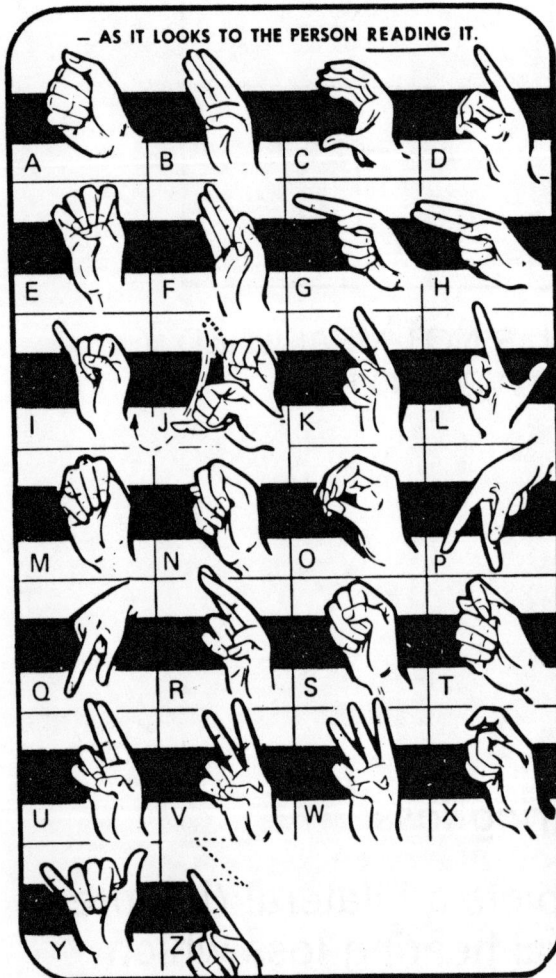

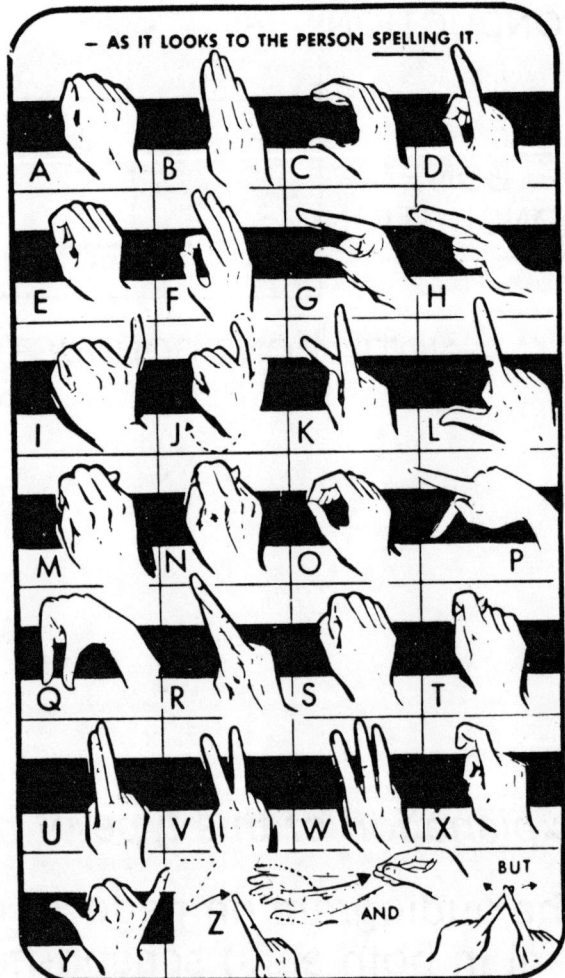

20

chapter 3

what you need to know to help the hearing impaired child in the regular classroom

WHAT IS IT LIKE TO BE HEARING IMPAIRED?

You can shut your eyes and imagine what it would be like to be blind, but you cannot completely block out sound and imagine what it is like to be hearing impaired.*

Confusion, misunderstanding, and the feeling of isolation are all areas that might disturb the hearing impaired child.

Getting Through is a record that describes what it sounds like to have different degrees of hearing loss. (See resource material, p. 105).

The hearing impaired person encounters serious problems when it comes to lipreading. Many of the phonemes or speech sounds such as (P, B, M) look the same to the hearing impaired person who is lipreading. Many sounds cannot be seen at all, such as (H, K, G, NG). Vowels seem to be the easiest sounds to lipread.

It has been estimated that less than 50% of a verbal message is decipherable on the lips. This infers that a good deal of skillful guesswork goes into speechreading.

WHEN DID THE HEARING LOSS OCCUR?

It is important to consider this question in order to understand the hearing impaired person's speech and language abilities.

The first three years of life are the most important for learning language and speech.

The later in the child's life the hearing loss occurs, the more capable the child is of understanding language.

If the hearing loss occurs post-lingually (i.e., after the basics of language have been absorbed), the hearing impaired person will have a language foundation.

Why is a language foundation important? We can look at the importance of a language foundation schematically.

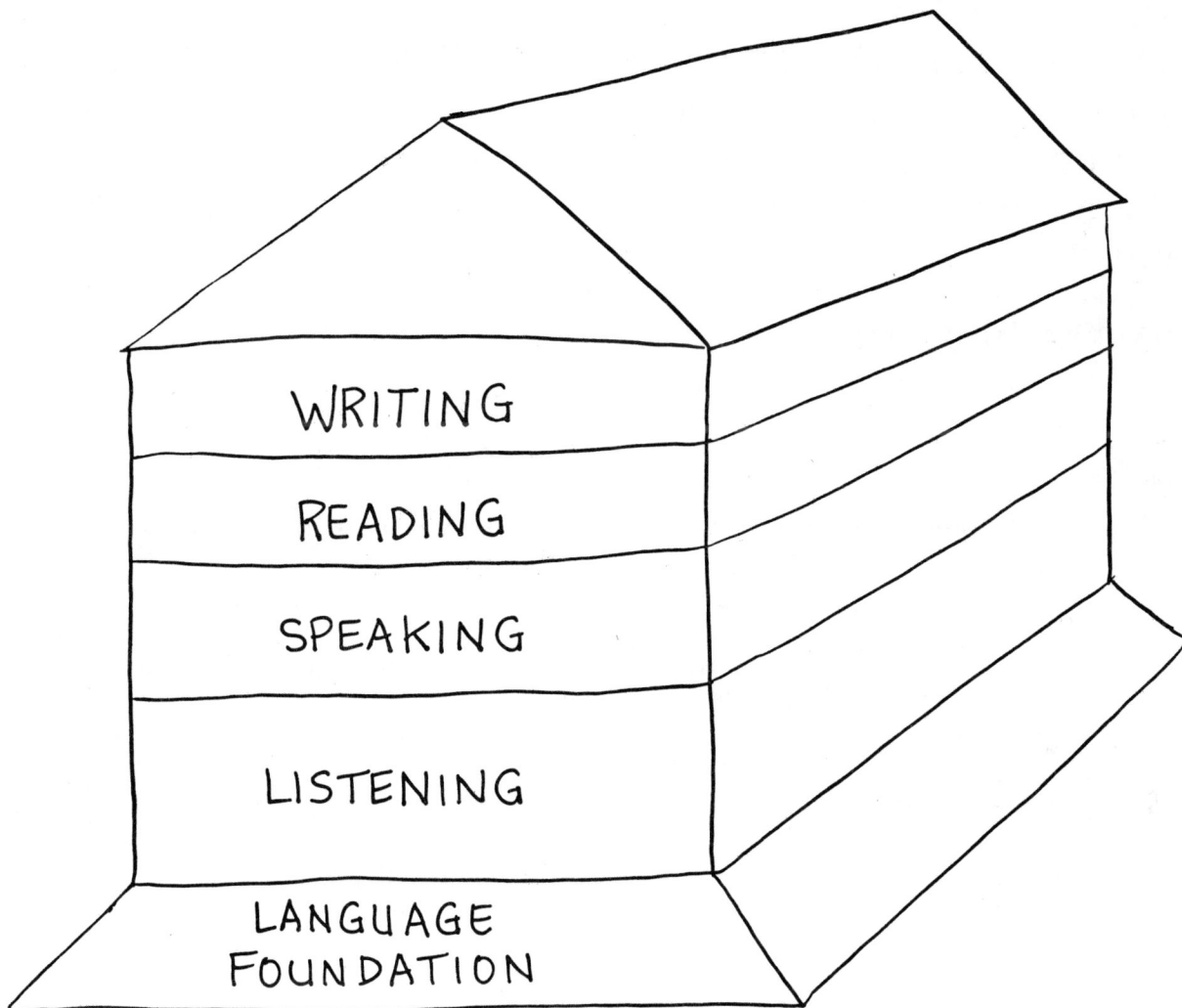

Each level of this "house" depends on a solid language foundation in order for communication to operate properly in its different forms.

AUDITORY EQUIPMENT

The Hearing Aid

The hearing aid is an instrument which brings amplified sound to the listener's ear. It is similar to a miniature public address system. There are two kinds of aids which the student may use: 1) the body aid and 2) the ear level aid.

1) The body aid

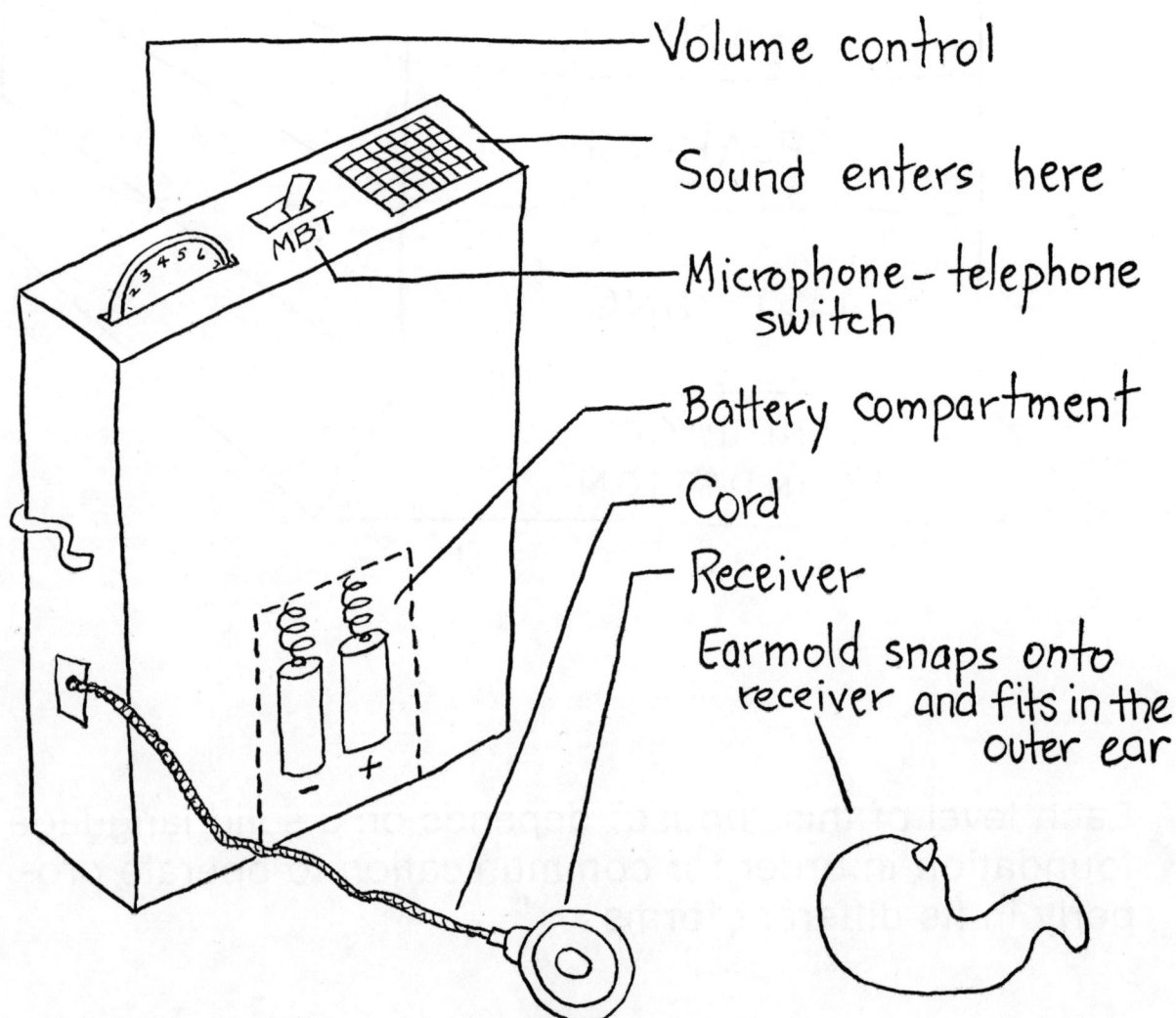

Volume control

Sound enters here

Microphone-telephone switch

Battery compartment

Cord

Receiver

Earmold snaps onto receiver and fits in the outer ear

2) The ear level aid

The ear level aid may be worn with the aid resting behind the ear in the arm of a pair of glasses, or it may be a separate aid worn behind the ear. Both types have a small plastic sound-conducting tube that connects the *receiver* to the *earmold.*

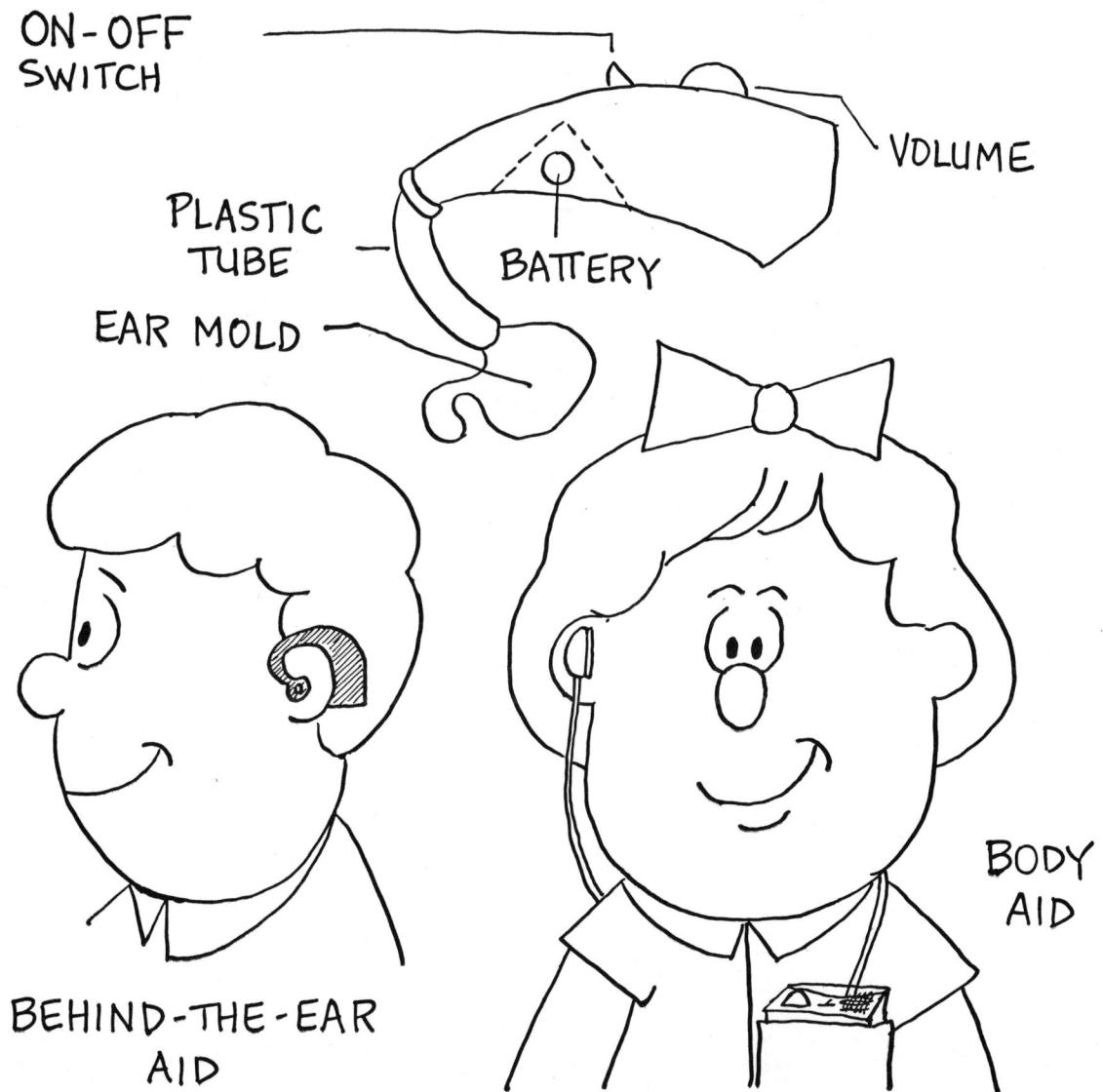

ON-OFF SWITCH

VOLUME

PLASTIC TUBE

BATTERY

EAR MOLD

BEHIND-THE-EAR AID

BODY AID

PARTS OF HEARING AID	FUNCTION OF PARTS	SPECIAL AREAS OF CONCERN
The Battery	Provides the power for the aid	Weak or worn-down batteries may be a cause of a poorly functioning aid. Replace the batteries and check the quality of the sound.
The Cord	Connects the hearing aid to the receiver. The cord is electrically insulated and flexible.	If the cord is frayed or worn, the sound from the receiver may be static or crackly.
The Earmold	Fits into the outer ear and is individually designed for the person's ear. The amplified sounds enter the ear through the opening in the earmold.	As children grow, the earmold will become loose and a whistle sound or "feedback" occurs. New molds need to be made periodically. A child wearing an aid may get an ear bumped while playing and this is painful. If there seems to be a lot of pain, get in touch with the otologist.
The Receiver	Is a button-like structure through which the amplified electric signal is converted back to a sound wave which is much louder than the original sound.	If the receiver is cracked or chipped the quality of sound may be poor.

The Microphone

When a microphone is available to the school, it can be worn by the teacher or by a student who wishes to communicate with the hearing impaired person. Since the microphone is usually light-weight, it can be worn indoors or outdoors on the playground, provided the hearing impaired student is within a certain radius of the speaker (this will depend on the type of microphone used).

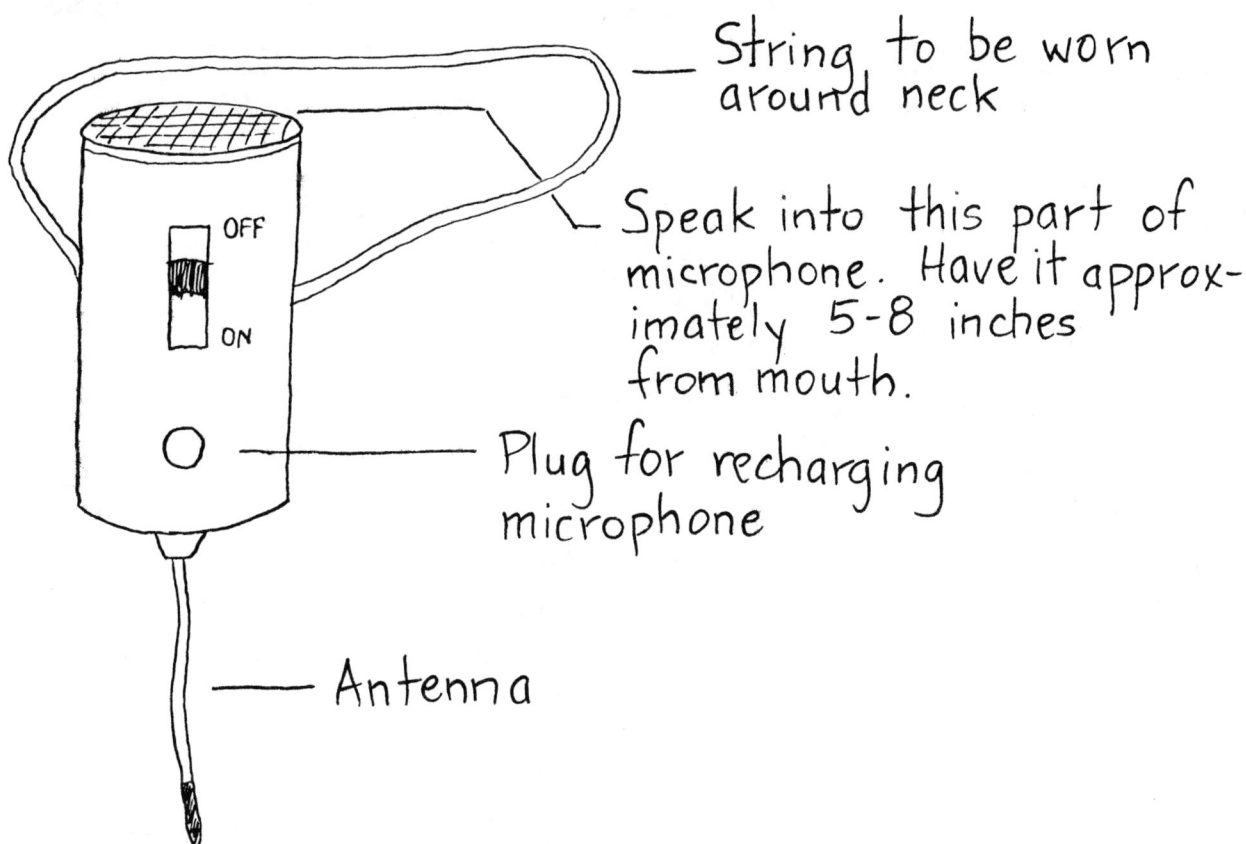

String to be worn around neck

Speak into this part of microphone. Have it approximately 5-8 inches from mouth.

Plug for recharging microphone

Antenna

This microphone is light-weight. The antenna is used to send the message to a companion hearing aid which the child will be wearing. Usually this kind of microphone will need to be recharged at the end of the day. There will be a special machine for this purpose. Extra supplies which are needed in the classroom include: batteries, receiver, earmold, and cord.

The teacher may be supplied with a microphone by the special education or itinerant teacher, who should instruct the classroom teacher on its use. Generally the type of microphone used is light-weight and worn near the mouth of the teacher. It can be clipped to a shirt or worn around the neck. The purpose of the microphone is to be in direct communication with the hearing impaired student. If students are giving oral presentations in class where the hearing impaired student is listening, the students should also be given the microphone as needed.

WARNING

Water or moisture ruins hearing aids, often beyond repair! If the aid is not in use, store in the hearing aid case and remove the batteries, lest corrosion take place inside the aid.

WARNING

The hearing aid should not be left in extreme temperatures, either too hot or too cold.

WARNING

If the hearing aid microphone is worn too close to the receiver, a squealing noise will be heard. This noise is called feedback, and while it may not bother the hearing impaired student, it may drive those around him to distraction!

WARNING

Always check to see that the hearing aid is turned off before it is taken off for the day.

SOCIAL DEVELOPMENT

The social maturity of the hearing impaired student often tends to be less than his or her hearing peers. Misunderstanding the nuances or subtleties of language contributes to this lack of social maturity. A tone of voice, a quick telling glance, regional expressions or vernacular are a few areas of communication that may escape a person who cannot hear.

"A thing or two" may need to be explained even though this expression is quite common. "Really" in this instance is a statement of affirmation, but it may also be a regional affectation.

Primarily, you should be aware of what you say and how you say it. Your tone of voice, the emphasis you put on certain words, and your facial and bodily expressions add meaning to oral language. Also, be conscious of the formation of the words the hearing impaired person will be lipreading (e.g. "make" and "bake" look the same to a lipreader).

SPECIAL CONSIDERATIONS

- Routine - your schedule

- Communication

- Classroom environment

- Feelings and expectations

ROUTINE - YOUR SCHEDULE

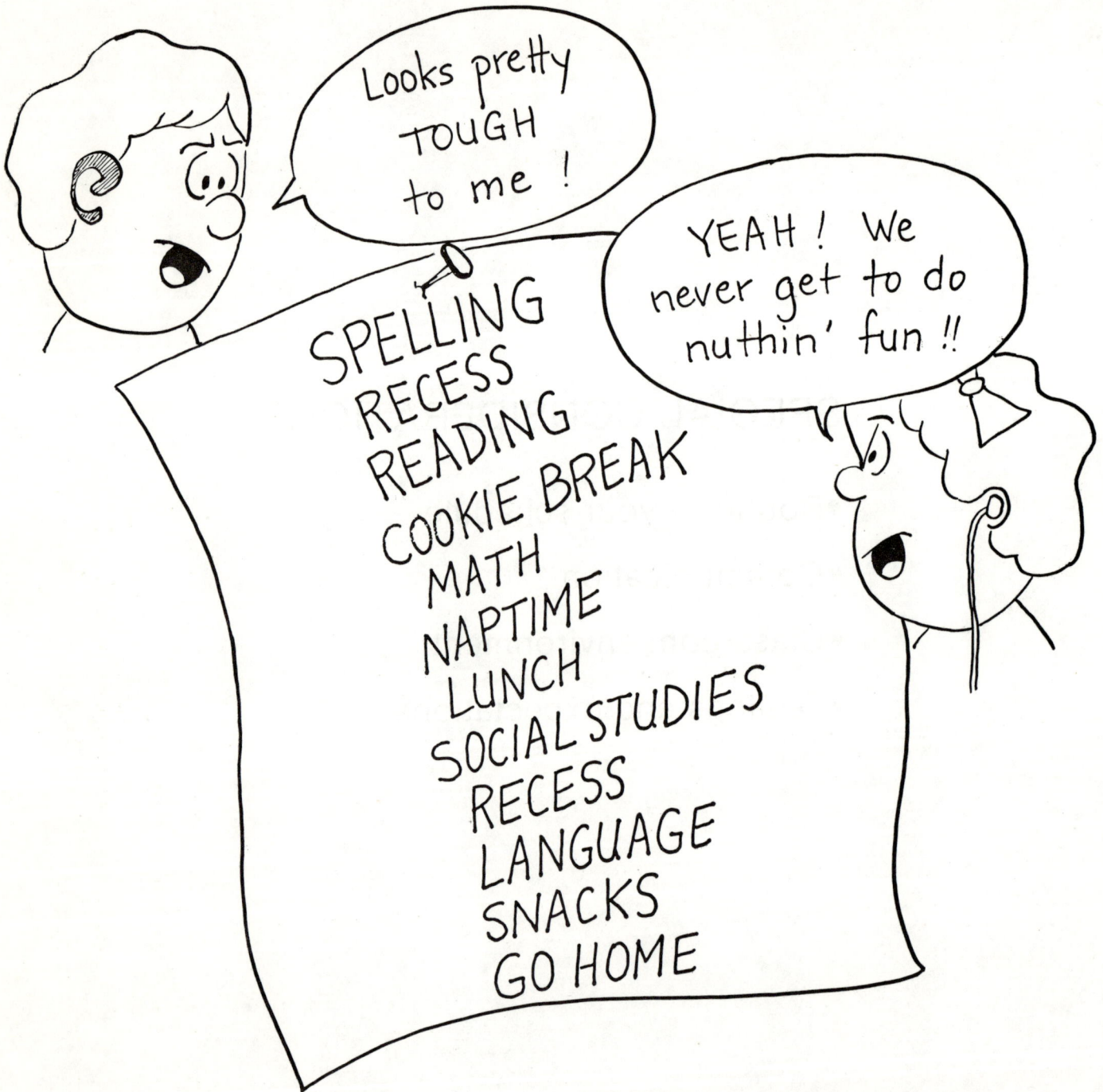

During the initial stages, follow a routine so that the hearing impaired person will know which activity should follow another activity.

The teacher will need to spend extra time with the hearing impaired student, with the special education or itinerant teacher, with the interpreter, and with the parents so that the student will not fall behind the rest of the class. A great deal of encouragement should be given to the student and realistic goals should be discussed and pursued.

COMMUNICATION

Talk facing the hearing impaired person.

Talk in complete, brief sentences and not in single words.

Speak with a pleasant and unstrained voice. Do not over-enunciate words because this will make the task of lip-reading more difficult.

Use natural gestures as you would use in talking with anyone else.

When talking about something or someone in the room,
glance, point, or walk over to the object and touch it.

If you want to get the attention of the hearing impaired
student and calling his or her name is not effective,
gently tap or touch the shoulder, arm, or hand of the
student. The idea is not to startle the person.

Do not assume the hearing impaired person has understood everything you have carefully explained, even if he or she nods and acknowledges understanding. Ask the hearing impaired student to explain the point you made to make sure your message was received properly.

Often another student can assist you in explaining something.

Supply diagrams and other visual aids whenever possible.

Key words, phrases, or new vocabulary should be 1) written on the chalkboard, 2) part of a permanent reference booklet, or 3) hanging on a chart holder where the class can refer to it when necessary.

Teachers could send home the reading material so that parents can explain new words to their child at home. By using the same word in different contexts, the hearing impaired student gradually learns the complexities and joys of understanding and using language. The parents could make a dictionary of new words using a loose-leaf binder so that the child could use it as a reference. The explanation of words should be written in terms the hearing impaired child understands.

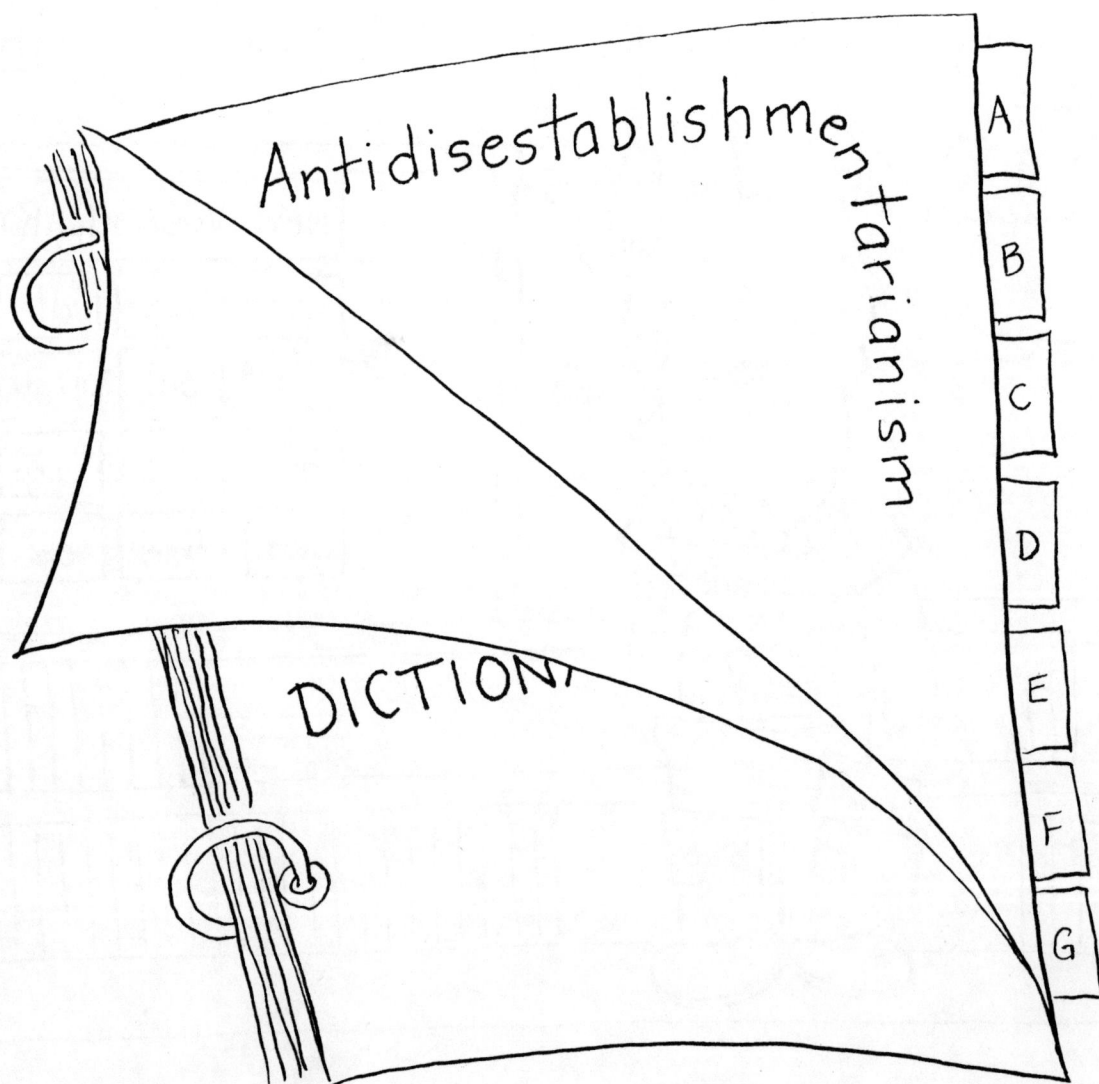

CLASSROOM ENVIRONMENT

Keep the noise level down since the hearing aid amplifies all sound and cannot sort out the important from the unimportant sounds.

If the room needs to be darkened for slides or films, make sure there is enough light on the face of the instructor so the hearing impaired student can follow any commentary or questions.

If there is an interpreter for the hearing impaired student, arrange for the interpreter to be seated next to the hearing impaired student.

Arrange for several student volunteers in class to be note-takers, as the hearing impaired student cannot take notes and watch the instructor at the same time without losing part or most of the message.

A tape recorder (preferably cassettes) may also be used if the hearing impaired student can arrange to have some-one transcribe the tape into written form.

The hearing impaired student should be seated in a central location, preferably in the middle of a semi-circular arrangement, and a couple of rows from the front so he or she will not have to strain to look up at the teacher.

Try to have as much natural light as possible illuminating the room. Fluorescent lights are harsh and tend to make lipreading much more difficult. The natural light should be on the face of the speaker so the hearing impaired student can lipread more easily. Lipreading is very difficult if the teacher is standing in front of the window while talking to a hearing impaired student.

Be aware of possible safety hazards in the areas where hearing would act as a signal or warning: e.g., fire alarm, traffic, or a cooking timer. Flashing lights can be installed to warn the hearing impaired person of a fire or other types of emergency drills.

FEELINGS AND EXPECTATIONS

Expect the same kind of behavior, responsibility, and dependability from the hearing impaired student as you would expect from the rest of the class.

Sometimes you may need to remind the hearing impaired student that he or she is mumbling or is making un-necessary noise, since this may disturb other students.

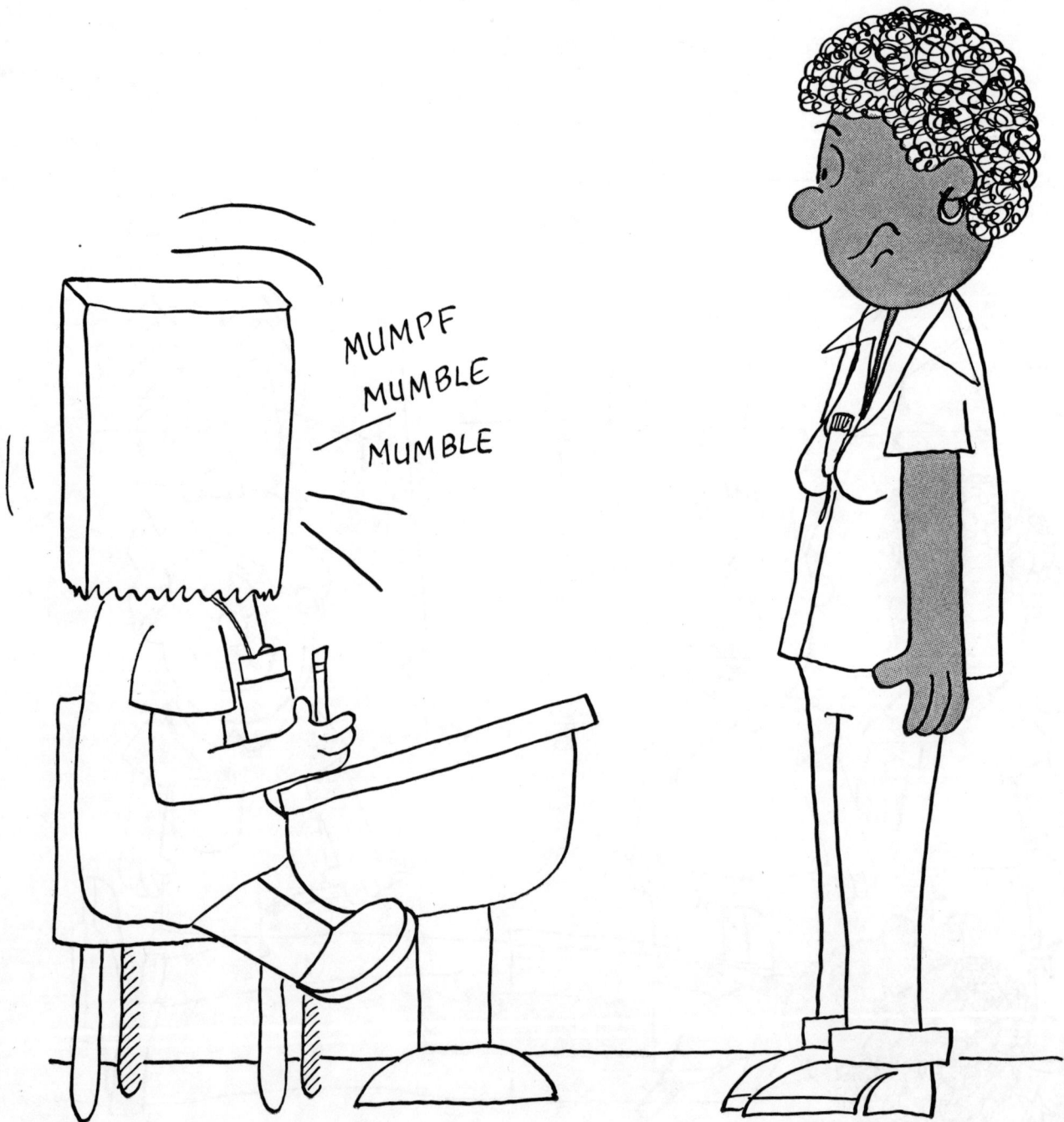

MUMPF
MUMBLE
MUMBLE

Do not be afraid to talk about handicaps. The chances are the hearing impaired person will be happy to answer questions which his or her curious classmates might have. Caution should be exercised with the hearing impaired student who is very self-conscious about his or her handicap.

TEACHING METHODS

- Experience trips & stories

- Vocabulary

- Reading

- Dramatic play

- Language of instruction

- Music

- Driver education

TEACHING METHODS

Hearing impaired students will have the most difficulty in subjects such as reading, creative writing, social studies, and probably extemporaneous speaking.

Today let's call upon Michael to speak to the class about our reading assignment... Michael? ... Michael?

To be successful in these areas a firm language base and language ability are necessary.

Mathematics, science, industrial arts. . .

. . .and home economics are a few areas where the hearing impaired person might excel since observation, figuring, and experimentation do not require an extensive use of language. Word problems in mathematics do pose difficulties when the wording is ambiguous. The teacher can rephrase a word problem so that it is clearly understood.

EXPERIENCE TRIPS AND STORIES

Experience is the best teacher and this is doubly true for the hearing impaired child.

If you are studying about farming, arrange for a trip to a farm. Take along a camera so you will have photographs of the experience which can later be put together in book form.

The hearing impaired student might be placed in charge of taking the photographs, since the pictures will be most helpful to him or her.

When the class returns to school you can write a story on a chart about what you saw and did. Later this chart can be reduced to booklet size and the photographs can be included.

VOCABULARY

Various subjects have special kinds of vocabulary for which the hearing impaired child may need explanations. Once again, a dictionary made for the hearing impaired student and written at the level of language comprehension he or she understands would be invaluable. Parents could help in this area.

The Indians were riding across the plain...

There is a math vocabulary, a science vocabulary, an industrial arts vocabulary, and so on. The written vocabulary is different from the spoken vocabulary. Common expressions and/or vernacular can be confusing to the hearing impaired person.

READING

Next to experience, reading is an excellent source of information. Newspapers are informative and are written in a crisp and understandable style.

Although comic books may be frowned upon by educators, some of the classic comic books can be very helpful for hearing impaired students. The pictures serve as an added clue to the meaning of the story, so reading becomes enjoyable and ceases to be a drudgery.

Reading helps to build language skills. The hearing impaired child should be encouraged to read, and in fact, should do more reading than hearing children. Parents can help their child at home in reading.

DRAMATIC PLAY

Experiences can be expressed imaginatively through dramatic play. Current events can be acted out. If you are fortunate enough to have a video machine, the students could present their version of a local or national news broadcast with details such as: headline news, weather, sports, and a local interest story. You may have the makings of a fine news team in your midst! The use of dramatic play can be an invaluable learning experience for the hearing impaired child.

THE LANGUAGE OF INSTRUCTION

The hearing impaired student may be discouraged with an assignment from the beginning if he or she cannot decipher the instructions. It is a good idea, therefore, to rephrase some of the more ambiguous instructions found on prepared exercises.

Underline the word that does not belong

Place an X beside the least full cup

Place an X on the ball that is bigger

Circle every other triangle

MUSIC

Hearing impaired people can enjoy rhythm and music. Although singing may not interest the hearing impaired student, . . .

. . .learning to play instruments can be challenging and fun.

Let the hearing impaired student be your guide as to what instrument he or she wishes to try. Teachers of hearing impaired children have noted a marked improvement in speech rhythm after the hearing impaired child learned to play an instrument. An audiogram may give a general picture of what the person hears on a given day with one kind of stimulus (e.g., white noise), but it cannot give an accurate picture of how the hearing impaired person *feels* while hearing and feeling sounds.

The senses of touch and hearing are both maximized while learning to play an instrument, and these sensations are usually pleasurable.

DRIVER EDUCATION

A conscientious teacher may be concerned about the hearing impaired student's driving.

There has been no documented correlation between hearing loss and accident rate. Hearing impaired people are usually very attentive and cautious drivers. In preparing for the written examination, it may be necessary to explain or reword some of the sample questions. Sometimes the written exams are worded in a way that would confuse a hearing impaired person.

The driver education instructor should collect a wide sample of tests given in the past in order to prepare the hearing impaired student for the types of questions asked.

chapter 4

**the mainstreaming story
of one child**

Joel was ten years old, hearing impaired, and fortunate enough to be in a school where he had extra help in language and speech. His special education teacher made arrangements for him to attend a regular class.

Joel's parents enthusiastically supported Joel's move from a classroom of hearing impaired children to the regular class.

Joel's special education teacher was trained to instruct hearing impaired children and was sensitive to the special needs he had. Joel's teacher and his parents visited his new class. They spoke with the teacher and principal of the school. This visit was made in the middle of the year prior to integration.

Joel's future teacher was understandably apprehensive about having a hearing impaired child in her class. She asked Joel's parents and special education teacher many questions. She wanted to be assured of receiving help for Joel and herself should they need it.

Joel's special education teacher made arrangements for an in-service training program late in the spring which would not only address Joel's new teacher's questions, but those of the entire staff as well.

The program,* which lasted several days, was geared to enlighten the staff regarding the special needs of the hearing impaired person. Teachers were interested in lipreading, sign language, and how to adapt teaching methods for a hearing impaired student. Joel's parents stimulated the greatest enthusiasm! They described what it was like to raise a hearing impaired child.

*In-service training kit (see resource materials).

Toward the end of the year, Joel was introduced to his future teacher and a few students took Joel around the school to get him acquainted with his new surroundings. Joel looked forward to seeing his new friends again and especially to getting into the swimming pool they had shown him!

Joel's parents and former special education teacher arranged for an itinerant teacher of hearing impaired children (i.e., one who travels to different schools in an area) to come to the school on a regular basis to answer any questions that might arise and to assist Joel when necessary.

Joel was very enthusiastic about his future placement. He asked his father if, during the summer, he could join the community swim club to get in shape for the fall. Maybe he could try out for the swim team at his new school! His father realized that this opportunity might "open the door" to making friends with future classmates, and gave Joel the "O.K.!"

Not all teachers have access to the same resources Joel's teacher had. If itinerant teachers are not available, the regular classroom teacher must teach the hearing impaired student by drawing on his or her own imagination and ingenuity.

Parents can be an invaluable source of strength and help to the teacher who has had little or no experience with hearing impaired children. Teachers and parents can be a mutually supportive team in helping the hearing impaired child reach his/her potential.

chapter 5

---

an ounce of prevention: early identification

The regular classroom teacher should be alert to identifying students with hearing problems. Some behaviors are indicative of a hearing loss.

- Difficulty following directions

After you finish your spelling, open up your reader and complete the exercises ... then take the language test before eating lunch.

Let's see ... Exercise your reader, and eat the spelling test. Something like that ... ... I think! Sounds strange doesn't it?

●Turning head to one side to hear better

●Not paying attention

• Hesitancy to participate in large groups, especially where a lot of talking takes place

•Discrepancy between observed ability of child and test scores

- Colds accompanied by earaches
- Problems in understanding speech after cold subsides

• Stubborn withdrawn behavior used as a defense mechanism by a hearing impaired child in order to protect his/her feelings of insecurity and isolation.

Now come on out of there Michael.

You must have the wrong wastebasket! Michael ain't in here!!

If a hearing loss is suspected, contact the child's parents or guardian and then the family physician. An audiologist should also be contacted if one is available. If not, inform the speech therapist or the school nurse.

In the case of wax build-up in the ear, swollen tonsils or adenoids, or an ear infection, the child should be referred to an otologist. This referral is usually made by the family physician, an audiologist, the school nurse, or the speech therapist.

REFERRAL SYSTEM

Teacher ⟶ Parents ⟶ Family physician ⟶ Otologist

chapter 6

**resources can make your
task easier**

RESOURCE PEOPLE

Parents can be your greatest resource!

Parents usually know their child's capabilities better than professionals do, and can be of assistance when it comes to evaluating the areas in which their child is either proficient or deficient.

Parents can transcribe tape recordings into note form so their hearing impaired child will have the same information as the rest of the class.

Parents can be part of a team effort to raise funds for new auditory equipment or other types of equipment for the classroom.

Parents may have special skills which they could share with the class. Woodworking, sewing, cooking, money management, dentistry, medicine, fire safety, special arts, and crafts are a fews skills that may be shared.

Parents may tutor other children who have specific difficulties.

There is usually no problem in obtaining parents' help unless they have other commitments. It is advisable for parents to work with children other than their own. Inhibition and frustration may discourage effective communication between a parent and his or her child in the classroom setting, but parents need to work with their own hearing impaired child at home.

Other resources might include:

- Psychologist
- Previous teachers
- Audiologist
- Otologist
- Family physician
- Clergy
- Speech and/or language therapist
- University programs that offer courses about the hearing impaired person
- Organizations serving the hearing impaired (see *American Annals* under resource material)
- Health and welfare agencies that may lend financial assistance to the hearing impaired student.

RESOURCE MATERIAL

I. Booklets:

    A. *Tim and His Hearing Aid* - Revised Edition
       By Eleanor Roonei and Joan Porter

       Alexander Graham Bell Association for the Deaf
       1537 Thirty-fifth Street, Northwest
       Washington, DC 20007

       This booklet describes a child who overcomes his apprehension about wearing a hearing aid.

    B. *The Girl Who Wouldn't Talk*

       International Association of Parents of the Deaf
       814 Thayer Avenue
       Silver Spring, MD 20910

       This booklet explains deafness to hearing children by telling a story about a little deaf girl who learns to talk through signs.

II. Films available from:

       Captioned Films for the Deaf Distribution Center
       5034 Wisconsin Avenue, Northwest
       Washington, DC 20016

III. Information on the hearing impaired available from the following sources:

    A. National Association of the Deaf
       814 Thayer Avenue
       Silver Spring, MD 20910

    B. Gallaudet College
       Kendall Green
       Washington, DC 20002

    C. The Volta Bureau
       1537 Thirty-fifty Street, Northwest
       Washington, DC 20007

    D. American Annals of the Deaf (Business Office)
       Directory of Programs and Services for the Deaf
       5034 Wisconsin Avenue, Northwest
       Washington, DC 20016

       This directory is divided into four main categories:

          I Educational Programs and Services
          II Rehabilitation Programs and Services
          III Community Programs and Supportive Services
          IV Research and Information Programs and Services

    E. Information for parents and teachers:

       Rights of the Handicapped
       Closer Look
       Post Office Box 1492
       Washington, DC 20013

IV. Record:

"Getting Through"

Zenith Radio Corporation
6501 West Grand Avenue
Chicago, IL 60635

This record describes what it sounds like to have differing degrees of hearing loss.

V. In-Service Training Information:

A. In-Service Training Program (Kit)
"Systems O.N.E." by G. B. Bitter

Educational Media Center
207 Milton Bennion Hall
University of Utah
Salt Lake City, UT 84112

B. Hi-Fi Program (Hearing Impaired Formal In-Service Training)

Center for Educational Media & Materials for the Handicapped
Ohio State University
Columbus, OH 43210

Contents: Manual, set of transparencies, audio cassette, video-tape recording

Purpose: For classroom teachers, school district personnel, and parents

VI. Book:

The Deaf Child in the Public Schools ($3.50)

I.A.P.D.
814 Thayer Avenue
Silver Spring, MD 20910

This book is written in a question and answer format.

chapter 7

---

conclusion

IT'S A PRIVILEGE

It *is* a privilege to have a hearing impaired student in your class for a number of reasons.

First of all, the teacher and class must unite in an effort to make the hearing impaired student feel accepted as a necessary part of the class. This kind of unity usually results in a class that is eager to participate and learn.

Second, unless you "live" with a person who must try harder than you do to achieve the same level of competency, it is difficult to realize how fortunate you are in having unimpaired senses. Teachers and students become more sensitive to each other. A hearing loss is then seen as an inconvenience and not as something to be pitied.

Third, the teacher(s) must be more precise and graphic in his or her teaching style in order to make the lesson clear and understandable to the hearing impaired pupil.

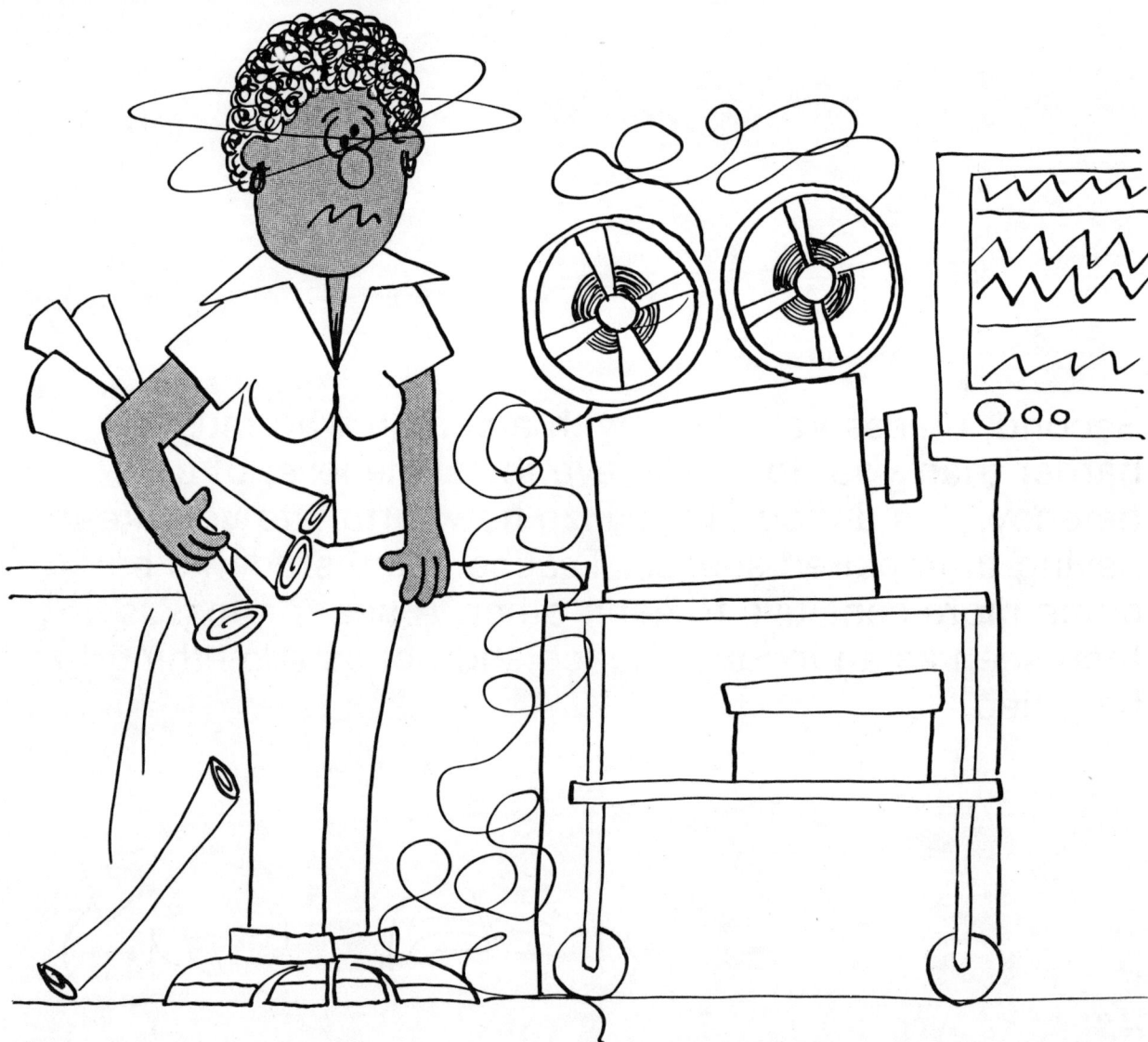

To speak precisely and clearly, it is also necessary to think clearly, and this is bound to benefit the entire class. Since the teacher serves as an example to the class, they in turn will make an effort to be more precise in their explanations and general conversation.

Self-scrutiny is not an easy undertaking, but the end result is usually self-understanding. By having a handicapped child in the regular classroom, you will be forced to examine your teaching style. You will need to adapt methods that have worked so well in the past with other children. You will be part of a team united to help the handicapped child and the rest of the class function as one.

You are at once the captain and part of the crew.

You are privileged!

BIBLIOGRAPHY

Berger, K. W. *The Hearing Aid: Its Operation and Development.* Detroit: National Hearing Aid Association, 1970.

Birch, J. W. *Hearing Impaired Children in the Mainstream.* Reston, V.A.: The Council For Exceptional Children, 1975.

Davis, H. & Silverman, S. R. *Hearing and Deafness.* New York: Holt, Rinehart and Winston, 1964.

Gearhardt, B. R. and Weishahn, M. W. *The Handicapped Child in the Regular Classroom.* Saint Louis: C. V. Mosby Company, 1976.

Northcott, W. H., (Ed.). *The Hearing Impaired Child in the Regular Classroom: Preschool Elementary, and Secondary Years.* Washington, DC: Alexander Graham Bell Association, 1973.

About the Editor

Thomas N. Fairchild has his Ph.D. in School Psychology and is currently an Assistant Professor of Guidance and Counseling and Coordinator of the School Psychology Training Program at the University of Idaho. Dr. Fairchild earned his Bachelors, Masters, and Specialist degrees at the University of Idaho. He received his Ph.D. from the University of Iowa in 1974. The editor has published over a dozen journal articles in the areas of school psychology and counseling. Dr. Fairchild has worked as a teacher, counselor, and school psychologist. He has had the privilege of working with students across all grade levels, and in his opinion they are all special.

About the Author

Janice Zatzman Orlansky received a Bachelor of Arts degree in Philosophy and English from Dalhousie University, Halifax, Nova Scotia, and a Master of Education of the Deaf (M.E.D.) from Smith College, Northampton, Massachusetts. She received a diploma from the Teacher Training Program, Clarke School for the Deaf, Northampton, Massachusetts.

She taught deaf children for three years and helped establish an integrated program for hearing impaired students in Halifax, Nova Scotia, Canada. For two years she taught deaf and language disordered children in Boston, Massachusetts.

Ms. Orlansky served for one year as the coordinator for public relations and volunteer services at the Seattle Hearing and Speech Center, Seattle, Washington.

For two years she was an instructor in the Department of Special Education, University of Idaho, Moscow, Idaho. She served as a member of a clinical evaluation team at the University of Idaho as well as a consultant to a program of integrated hearing impaired students in Lewiston, Idaho. She is currently engaged in private practice in language therapy in Charlottesville, Virginia.

About the Illustrator

Everyone can draw—some with more competence than others. Occasionally you find someone who is exceptionally gifted in a particular facet of drawing. Danial B. Fairchild is that someone. He is a highly talented cartoonist with a style that is uniquely his own. Among his achievements include cartoons printed in newspapers and magazines, and most recently two paperbacks entitled **Cowtoons** (Artcraft Press, Nampa, Idaho), which depict in a very humorous way the life of cowboys.